Also from Westphalia Press
westphaliapress.org

Reports on British Prison-Camps in India and Burma

Visited by the
International Red Cross Committee in
February, March and April, 1917

by the International Committee of the Red Cross

WESTPHALIA PRESS
An Imprint of Policy Studies Organization

Reports On British Prison-Camps In India And Burma: Visited By The International Red Cross Committee In February, March, And April, 1917

Westphalia Press
An imprint of Policy Studies Organization
1527 New Hampshire Ave. NW
Washington, D.C. 20036
info@ipsonet.org

ISBN-13: 978-1-63391-788-0
ISBN-10: 1-63391-788-6

Cover design by Jeffrey Barnes:
jbarnesbook.design

Daniel Gutierrez-Sandoval, Executive Director
PSO and Westphalia Press

Updated material and comments on this edition can be found at the Westphalia Press website:
www.westphaliapress.org

REPORTS ON BRITISH PRISON-CAMPS IN INDIA AND BURMA

VISITED BY THE INTERNATIONAL RED CROSS COMMITTEE IN FEBRUARY, MARCH AND APRIL, 1917

NEW YORK
GEORGE H. DORAN COMPANY
MCMXVIII

PRICE, TEN CENTS

INTRODUCTION

Early this year the British camps in India and Burma for Turkish prisoners of war and civil residents in the Indian Empire of enemy nationality, were visited by three accredited representatives of the International Committee of the Red Cross at Geneva. These three gentlemen—MM. F. Thormeyer, Em. Schoch and Dr. F. Blanchod—spent over three months on their commission, landing at Bombay on February 12th and sailing from Colombo on May 20th.

The conclusions they reached are presented in an article by M. Thormeyer and an official report addressed by them jointly to the International Committee.

The report is nearly a hundred pages long, and gives a systematic account of each camp visited under a number of heads:—Altitude and climate; number and category of prisoners; number of staff, with names of responsible officers; specifications of housing and sleeping accommodation; exercise; rations; clothing; hygiene; washing; lighting; water supply, sanitary arrangements and disinfection; medical attendance; hospitals (with specifications as above); discipline; amusements; postal correspondence and censorship; parcels; remittances; relief of destitution; previous inspection by neutral representatives; mosques, churches and religious services. The different sections are supplemented by statistical tables, and the same detailed treatment is given to all the ten camps of the kind which have been established in British Indian territory: the camp at Sumerpur, for Christian and Mohammedan prisoners of war from the Turkish army (mostly of non-Turkish race); the camp at Ahmednagar, for interned civilians; the camp at Belgaum, for women and children of enemy nationality; the camp at Bellary, for Turkish prisoners of war; the depôt-camp at Calcutta; the camp for interned civilians at Katapahar; the camp at Thayetmyo, in Burma, for Turkish prisoners of war (mostly of Turkish race); the camp for convalescents at Shwebo; the new camp at Meiktila; and the quarantine camp at Rangoon.

Many of the facts given in this report are of an almost purely technical interest, and the translation and publication of the whole would be a considerable task. On the other hand, the general impressions of the three Commissioners are of great interest, and there are a number of special observations in the body of the report which deserve publication in a more accessible form.

Accordingly a translation is here given of M. Thormeyer's article practically as it stands, with a few omissions for the sake of greater brevity. And short extracts are added from the full report, where the latter seems to add materially to M. Thormeyer's description.

In making extracts there is always a danger of producing a one-sided impression, but care has been taken here to select unfavorable as well as favorable judgments of the Commissioners, as far as possible in the proportion in which they stand to each other in the original.

CONTENTS

BRITISH PRISON CAMPS IN INDIA AND BURMA

Article by M. F. Thormeyer, one of the three Red Cross Commissioners

. . . Since the beginning of the war the International Committee of the Red Cross of Geneva has concentrated a great deal of its energy on dealing with that very important and painful matter—the lot of prisoners of war. The Prisoners of War Agency instituted at Geneva has been at work for almost three years, rendering invaluable aid to prisoners and their families. . . .

The International Committee has also organized visits of inspection to prisoners' camps in the belligerent countries. The governments of the various countries have recognized the importance of such visits, which, being undertaken by competent and impartial persons, have, as a result of first-hand investigations, yielded exact information on a subject that is treated in the press and elsewhere with more feeling than justice.

During the early months of 1917 the International Committee sent a delegation to the prisoner-of-war camps in Egypt, India and Burma. The report on Egyptian camps made by this delegation has been published at Geneva, and that on Indian camps will soon be issued. It will certainly be read with interest in this country (Switzerland) as well as in England. While awaiting its publication we are able to give some information about this expedition and its results, which will no doubt be welcomed by our readers.

The Swiss Mission consisted of MM. Dr. F. Blanchod, F. Thormeyer and E. Schoch. The first of these had already visited the German prisoners in Morocco and French prisoners in Germany. M. Thormeyer had been to the camps in Germany, Russia, Siberia and Turkestan. These earlier expeditions enabled the delegates to set up standards for comparing the treatment accorded to prisoners in the different countries. The mission arrived in Egypt at the end of December, 1915, and visited the camps at Maadi, Sidi-Bisch and Bilbéis, the internment premises in the Cairo Citadel, and the hospitals and internment camp for German civilian prisoners at Ras-el-Tin. As the report on the Egyptian camps is already in print, we refer our readers to it. . . .

MM. Blanchod, Schoch and Thormeyer reached Bombay on February 12. . . .

The Indian Government received them with the greatest courtesy, treated them as distinguished guests throughout their stay, and afforded them all possible facilities for fulfilling their mission. The Viceroy of India offered them hospitality and showed how deeply interested he was in the purpose of their expedition. While at Delhi, the delegates were put in touch with the civil and military authorities and most kindly welcomed by them. So that they should travel more comfortably in a strange country, a very distinguished English officer was attached to them. Thanks to his knowledge of India, and especially of means of communication and of local customs, he was able to relieve them of all the worries and anxieties which might have made their task a difficult one.

The delegates were subjected to no restrictions during their camp inspections. They had free access to all camps and places of internment—a privilege not granted them elsewhere, and full liberty to question the prisoners privately, examine registers and reports, and return several times to the same camp to receive petitions and complaints. The British authorities recognized that the purpose of these visits was to obtain all possible improvements in the conditions in which the prisoners lived, asked the delegates to communicate to them all their observations, and gave serious consideration to whatever was suggested. In India prisoner-of-war camps come into the sphere of the military authorities, while those for interned civilians are controlled by the civil Governments of the Presidencies in which they are respectively situated.

The first camp visited by the Swiss Mission was that at Sumerpur, which contains some thousands of Turkish prisoners. After leaving Eninpura station, one crosses a large plain bordered by rocky hills and intersected by a river which dries up during the hot season. A barbed-wire fence surrounds a huge quadrangle, in which the huts occupied by the Turks and the administrative buildings are arranged in several parallel rows. It is a small town with wide streets, buildings of one type, its own lighting, water, and drainage systems, a provision market, a postal service, etc. The general impression it leaves is a strange one; no women or children are to be seen, only men clad in more or less fancy uniforms, spending their days in idleness. Except at meal times, when a crowd flocks round the kitchens and messing places, little animation is apparent. Seated under the verandahs running round each hut, groups of prisoners play with dice or dominoes, or converse while drinking cup after cup of Turkish coffee. The news given in the English papers, politics, or camp tittle-tattle forms the subject of discussion. The many nationalities of which the Turkish army is composed form separate groups, which are not particularly well disposed toward one another.

The arrival of the delegates was a great event amid the monotony of camp life. These gentlemen visited the huts, counted the sleeping mats and blankets, inspected the lavatories, baths and latrines; went to the kitchens to check the rations and to the canteens to learn prices; tasted the water, bread, meat and coffee; stopped a long time in the post offices, and passed some hours in the infirmaries and hospital. The prisoners were then drawn up by sections. Every section contained men who had some knowledge of a language other than Turkish —French, English, German, or even Russian. These acted as spokesmen for their comrades. Each camp has its interpreters, but wherever possible prisoners are communicated with directly. The delegates, standing in the blazing sunshine, listened to complaints and requests, took notes, made counter-inquiries, and wrote down names, dates and addresses. With the help of their improvised dragomans, they questioned a great number of soldiers. This procedure was repeated for each section. The more important cases were summoned to the camp office and examined at greater leisure. Complaints were then classified under headings and discussed with the camp authorities. It requires much practice and discrimination to pick out such complaints as have any solid foundation. A prisoner, in whatever country he may be, complains because he suffers. The loss of freedom upsets his sense of proportion. A porter from Constantinople or a fisherman from the Black Sea coast, though he draws every day the same rations as a British soldier, manages to complain about his food. In districts where mutton is the staple meat, beef is asked for; where beef is the rule, everybody wants mutton. Bitter complaints were made about correspondence. "I get no news of my family," is a phrase that one heard constantly. The prisoner who got no letters assumed that the postal service was no good. Others were worried about the trade they had lost, their ruined businesses, their lands going to waste. Each one had his troubles. It was a trial to the delegates themselves to listen to all these tales of woe, which they could not alleviate, and to have nothing to offer but a few words of comfort and encouragement.

Their chief task was to make sure that the treatment accorded to the prisoners of war conformed with international regulations, and that rules laid down regarding housing, hygiene, clothing, food, work, medical attention, correspondence, etc., were conscientiously observed. Their investigations were concerned chiefly with the general conditions of the prisoners in each camp. Hospital registers were consulted carefully, as being the surest means of gauging the effect of the climate on the prisoners' health. Generally speaking, prisoners always found the climate of the place in which they were interned horrible. Here the heat was complained of, there the damp, there the dryness, somewhere else the rain, and so on. As the prisoners' camps were in all cases in cantonments selected for British troops, and the disease and death rates among prisoners were no higher than those of British soldiers—and invariably lower than those of the native population—one naturally concluded that the Indian climate, though enervating and exhausting in the long run, did not have bad effects on the general health of the prisoners.

During the journey—often a long one—from one camp to another, the delegates classified their notes, drew up their reports and conducted correspondence about their work. Leaving Sumerpur, they proceeded to Ahmednagar, a large concentration camp for interned German and Austrian civilians. The two other civilian camps, at Belgaum in the south and Katapahar in the north, were also visited.

It was impossible not to feel genuinely sorry for the interned civilians. Most of them had bèen several years in India, engaged in business, managing prosperous commercial firms or enjoying well-paid employment. They had become used to the free, comfortable Indian life; several had married English wives; and some were, or believed themselves to be, naturalised. To have to leave their pretty bungalows for the internment camp, give up business, see their future compromised and their interests endangered, was truly hard to endure; and explains the complaints which they insisted on getting through to their native countries. It was all very well to remind them that the same state of things prevailed in all belligerent countries and that the evils of war affected hundreds of thousands of men more terribly—their reply was that other people's sufferings did not make their own any the easier to bear.

The internment of civilians is one of the measures enforced by warfare. It would be unjust to add unnecessary harshness to what is a stern necessity. The British Government makes a point of reducing the inconveniences of internment to a minimum by allowing all ameliorations that are consistent with the rules. Although few of the interned frankly recognised that their treatment is as good as circumstances permit, a thorough investigation showed that conditions of housing, hygiene, and food were excellent; that means of occupying and amusing the prisoners were well thought out; that the interned were treated with the greatest kindness, and that such complaints as there were related in most cases to matters over which the camp commandants had no control. It was a real satisfaction to delegates who had visited concentration camps in some other countries to see clean, spacious and convenient quarters, provided with bathrooms, to visit kitchens both well ordered and plentifully equipped, to find concert and lecture halls and a theatre, to watch games of tennis and football, gymnastic exercises and fencing, and, above all, to be able to convince themselves *de visu* that the appearance and bearing of the interned argued good treatment.

At Belgaum, where the internees' families are settled, every quarters had the appearance of a comfortably furnished family home. Pretty furniture, carpets, pictures, books and pianos, with which the interned were allowed to provide themselves, gave the impression of home life. Internees free to take walks in the surrounding country seemed like visitors on holiday rather than enemy subjects in captivity. An English school received children free. The interned were even allowed to run a school at their own expense under a German mistress. In this place, too, there was grumbling—the sums allotted were too small, private affairs were conducted on sufferance, news came too seldom, etc. Visiting the bazar was forbidden for reasons of health; so of course everybody wished to go to it. At the bottom of all these complaints were the usual miseries of human existence, aggravated by boredom and the loss of liberty.

When one thinks of all the difficulties which the Government has to face in accommodating and guarding interned civilians, one realises that the exchange of the last would be a real relief to the authorities, if the problem were not beset by insurmountable difficulties. However, it is certain that a good number of the interned wish to stay in India, and regard a return to their native country as the greatest disaster that could happen to them.

After spending two months on visiting the Indian camps, the Swiss delegates left for Burma. Some important camps had been formed there specially for Turkish prisoners sent from Mesopotamia. For several months past their number had increased considerably.

To transport prisoners so great a distance demanded very careful organisation. Specially equipped boats take convoys from Busra to Kurachi, whence they are carried by rail to Calcutta. A depôt camp in this town receives the prisoners for several days, during which they undergo a medical inspection, additional to those made at the point of embarkation. A steamer then transfers them to Rangoon. On their arrival at that port they are inspected again. The sick and suspected cases are detained in a special hospital; the other prisoners are put aboard large lighters towed by steamers of the I. N. C. The small flotilla ascends the Irrawaddy. According to the situation of the camp the convoys reach it directly by boat or complete the journal to it by rail.

Thayetmyo is a large camp on the right bank of the Iraawaddy. The splendid mango trees, which give the place its name, shelter many pagodas whose white spires rise above the dark foliage. The high banks command the great spread of river, which at low water exposes some sandy islands. In the distance a chain of blue-tinted mountains bounds the horizon.

On the day of their arrival the delegates were present at a gymkhama organised by the Turkish prisoners, and held on a huge rectangle of turf surrounded by fine trees. On one side was a marquee for notabilities—the camp authorities, Turkish officers, people invited from the town, and even some ladies. The Turkish soldiers crowding round the other three sides formed a living hedge. Races, jumping and boxing events and various other sports drew applause or laughter from the crowd. The winners came before the judging committee and received prizes in money from the Turkish Colonel S——. The prisoners, taken out of themselves by the physical exercise and encouraged by the cheering, lost the lazy and tired look which is often produced by idleness. They were stoutly built fellows with a soldierly bearing, keen eyes and lissom and proud carriage. The sports were to last three evenings, but the delegates, to their great regret, could be present at only one meeting, since all their time was taken up with work.

The population of the camp was a mixed one. Even among the officers very different elements could be distinguished. The delegates noticed here, as in other countries, that the higher their rank the more moderate are the officers in their opinions, and the better do they appreciate the real kindness with which they are treated. Some of the younger officers, whose education had obviously been neglected, made bitter and violent complaints. But the great majority expressed themselves as satisfied.

The soldiers were unanimous in asserting that they are well treated. But since the opportunity of laying their little troubles before the Red Cross delegates was too precious to be wasted, they made use of it, and long sessions were spent on listening to grievances, among which the money question took first place. Still, their stories showed no ill-feeling towards their guards. They had suffered in the war and been separated from their families, while their business had gone to the dogs; but that was fate and nobody's fault. Their Oriental fatalism keeps them from becoming uselessly excited.

The regrettable idleness of the camps affects them hardly at all. If given work, they performed it obediently with an eye to earning a little money; nevertheless, they liked to spend their days in their own way.

The camp authorities have allotted them a building

to serve as mosque, and imams come to hold services. There is little religious keenness, and many of the men are indifferent.

Speaking generally, the behaviour of the Turkish prisoners is good, and serious offences are rare. There is a noticeable increase in the breaking of disciplinary rules whenever new elements from the front come to camp. But after a few days these newcomers fall into line. Punishment is meted out with the strictest justice and all possible humanity; and the delegates received no complaints as to prisoners being brutally or violently handled. . . .

The most lasting impression left on the delegates' memory sums up the many exhaustive observations made during their visit to the prisoners' camps. The delegates are of the opinion that the British are to-day treating their prisoners as if they were to be their friends in the more or less near future. The care lavished on their welfare, the constant desire to improve their lot, and the absence of useless annoyances are the factors in a treatment which conforms with the principles of humanity and civilisation and does honour to the British race. Furthermore, this is a wise line of action to take, since barbarity and cruelty exercised over long periods create an impassable gulf between belligerents, and, while outraging humanity, constitute a grievous political error. . . .

Extracts from the Report of the Three Commissioners to the International Red Cross Committee at Geneva

1. CAMP AT SUMERPUR (RAJPUTANA)

Visited 3-4 March, 1917. Contained 3,366 Turkish prisoners of war, mostly Moslems, among whom Mesopotamian Arabs predominated.

. . . In the Sumerpur Camp are two muftis and two judges who act as priests (imams), but do not mix with the officers. Almost all civilians are liable to military service, the only exceptions being governers, judges, heads of religion and some of the higher officials, members of the Parquet. . . .

Food. The feeding arrangements at Sumerpur Camp are based on the principle—which we found to be a very good one—of entrusting the prisoners with the preparation of their own meals. Especially in the East, where matters relating to food have in almost all cases a religious significance, this procedure has the double advantage of pleasing the prisoners and relieving the camp authorities of many complaints and difficulties. We consider that this method, which shows a practical broad-mindedness, should be adopted in all prisoner camps. The following incident will serve as an example of the scrupulous care taken by the British to avoid anything that might offend the religious susceptibilities of other races. As Sumerpur Camp is situated in Rajputana, an independent Hindoo state wherein cows and oxen are regarded as sacred animals, beef is never allowed to appear on the table of the commandant and camp officials.

Every morning the section sergeants and men on fatigue duty go to the hall where rations are drawn. This is a very well constructed circular building, surrounded by arcades with walls about four feet high. Inside is a corridor containing scales. The provisions are brought from an adjoining store and placed on a stone table which is kept scrupulously clean. The rations, apportioned according to a scale posted in the place and to the number of men in a section, are delivered to the orderlies and taken by them to the section kitchens, to be prepared there by cooks elected by the prisoners themselves.

The following table shows the prisoners' daily individual rations:—

Wheat meal (atta)	453.6 gr.	(1 lb.)
Rice	226.8 "	(½ lb.)
Lentils (dall)	85.0 "	
Melted butter (ghee)	28.35 "	
Vegetables	226.8 "	(½ lb.)
Potatoes (instead of vegetables)	113.4 "	(¼ lb.)
Onions	56.70 "	(2 oz.)
Salt	23.27 "	
Sugar	31.03 "	
Tea	7.75 "	
Firewood	1360.0 "	(3 lbs.)
Meat (goat)	186.18 "	
Seasoning (tumeric)	4.0 "	

All these provisions are supplied by native contractors and inspected for appearance, quality and quantity by the British authorities. We were able to satisfy ourselves that the materials delivered for the prisoners' use is of first-class quality. What is more, in the course of an enquiry among the prisoners, we received no complaints about food. . . .

In addition to food rations, each prisoner receives one pound of soap monthly, and 40 cigarettes and two boxes of matches weekly. It is interesting to note that, in the case of some articles, the prisoners' rations are larger than those of the British soldiers of the guard. . . .

We received no complaints with regard to clothing. As a concession to Eastern customs the prisoners are allowed great latitude in their dress and headgear. At Sunday morning parade we noticed the greatest possible variety in the men's apparel:—military tunics, civilian waistcoats, smocks, long cotton robes, Turkish frock-coats, fezzes, turbans, caps, slouch hats, embroidered skull-caps, etc. Every prisoner has a small tin identity disc, but it need not be worn on the clothes, and most of the prisoners carry it in a pocket. The footwear preferred by prisoners is the Eastern slipper. To sum up, the prisoners' clothing is ample, clean, comfortable and suited to their tastes.

Medical attention. The camp medical service is in the hands of Captain Wadia, an Indian doctor, who qualified at Saint Bartholomew's Hospital, London. He is assisted by two native doctors, health officers with the right to practise medicine in India but not in England. . . .

The doctor-captain speaks Arabic and Persian. Two Armenians acting as interpreters speak French, English and Arabic. At the present time there is under discussion the possibility of procuring a camp dentist from Bombay, half the cost being borne by the British authorities and half by the civilian prisoners who require his services. . . .

All the equipment is kept in very good order: A surgeon's chest, an optician's chest, a chest for forceps, and sterilising apparatus. A microscope is employed continually on making analyses. There is a plentiful supply of medicines. The hospital was opened in July, 1915, at the same time as the camp. The general health of the camp may be regarded as good, considering that many of the prisoners arrive in a very weak state, greatly exhausted by the Mesopotamia campaigns. . . .

All the men were inoculated, like the British and native soldiers, against cholera and smallpox, but not against typhoid, since no case of that disease has been identified among the prisoners in the camp. . . .

Death rate. In addition to the 13 cases mentioned above there were, in 1916, 31 deaths from non-epidemic diseases, making a total of 44 deaths for 1916, or a death rate of exactly 1 per cent. A comparison with the rates verified by us in prisoner camps of various belligerent countries shows that the mortality is very low at Sumerpur.

To complete the figures we will add that there were 16 deaths during the six months of 1915. The deceased prisoners were buried according to the rites of their religion. . . .

Discipline. The attitude of the commandant and officers of the guard towards the prisoners seemed to us to be excellent. The prisoners are guarded by 40 British and 225 Indian soldiers. We received no complaints about treatment from any of the many prisoners to whom we spoke through the medium of an interpreter. All expressed themselves as well satisfied with their food, quarters and treatment. No cases of bodily violence or brutality were brought to our notice. . . .

Disciplinary punishment. The following regulations apply to all camps for prisoners in India. The camp commandant alone has the right to inflict any kind of punishment. No prisoner may be punished without first being informed of the charge brought against him and being allowed to make his defence. The commandant may commit to cells for a period not exceeding 14 days. While in confinement the prisoner is on the reduced scale of rations, No. 2. But no prisoner may be sent to the cells or be put on reduced rations for more than 24 hours without the express sanction of the camp medical officer.

Imprisonment is in the camp cells. A prisoner who has been confined for 14 days may not be sent back to the cells until 7 days have elapsed. Prisoners in the cells may be given permission to work; and are allowed to take walking exercise for at least two hours daily.

As light punishments the commandant may forbid prisoners to smoke or take part in camp amusements, withhold money from them, give them the hardest fatigue duties, and restrict the receiving or sending of letters. . . .

Quarrels, theft and the sale of things provided by the administration are the most usual causes of punishment. There has been no attempt to escape from camp. . . .

Religion and recreation. The prisoners are quite free to practise their religion, and have a small mosque in which imams read the Koran. Occasionally a French monk comes to the camp to celebrate mass for the Christians.

The Armenian, Bishop of Cairo, Mgr. Thorgom Koushaguian, visited the camp on Christmas Day, 1916. Music and singing are allowed. The Armenians lately sent home had got together quite a good orchestra.

All kinds of games are permitted. Orientals prefer backgammon, dominoes and card games to sports. Most of the prisoners are illiterate. Some of the better educated civilians read to them from the Koran and the papers.

Correspondence; money orders. The average monthly total value of money orders is 2,000 rupees (1 rupee = fr. 1.65). Most of these orders come from Mesopotamia, being but a very short time in transmission, while those sent through the Turkish Red Cross are two months on the way. A prisoner may have all the money sent him in one sum; and some civilians have received as much as 500 rupees at a time. No deductions are made. The amounts are paid at the official rate of exchange. Prisoners sign receipts, which are sent to Turkey. Illiterates make a thumb-mark on the receipt. Anyone who does not wish to have all the money at once has an account opened in his name, showing deposits, drawings and receipts.

Parcels. On the average, about fifteen parcels arrive weekly from Mesopotamia, and about as many from Europe through the Prisoners-of-War International Agency of the Red Cross at Geneva. As a rule they reach the camp in good condition: only those from Mesopotamia are opened before delivery. Alcohol, ether, scents and newspapers are forbidden.

Letters and postcards. Prisoners may write one

letter per week, in any language and of any length. Letters are censored by the interpreter in the camp itself. Prisoners are also allowed to send postcards, but avail themselves less of this means of correspondence.

The authorities supply notepaper and envelopes free of cost. . . .

About 50 per cent. of the prisoners have had news of their families since reaching camp, although news usually comes only at long intervals. Prisoners taken at Mardin* (Mesopotamia) have heard nothing of their families and assert that the latter have all been massacred by the Turks. . . .

We did not consider it necessary to distribute relief, though at the commandant's suggestion we made two exceptions. The first was a civilian prisoner, an Armenian journalist from Egypt, quite destitute, to whom we sent 50 rupees; the second, a blind old man from Basrah, to whom we sent 20 rupees.

---

*The Commissioners evidently misunderstood their informants, who were Armenian inhabitants of Mardin, but were not made prisoners there. Mardin lies in N. Mesopotamia, far behind the present Turkish front. The Armenian population was massacred in 1915.

2. CAMP AT AHMEDNAGAR (BOMBAY PRESIDENCY)

Visited 7 March, 1917. Contained 1,621 persons, of whom 452 were military (apparently including captured crews of German ships), the rest civilians. The camp was divided into three separate sections, A and B (to which prisoners were assigned according to social class), and C for those who had given their parole.

. . . *Housing.* The internment camp at Ahmednagar comprises a large number of buildings, some of which had already been used as quarters for troops, while the rest were erected specially for the internees. In Camp C, the parole camp, the interned are housed in three large dressed stone buildings, with wide verandahs. Four officers have to themselves a pretty bungalow, surrounded by greenery and flowers. In Camp B, the usual form of hutment is a building measuring 150 by 60 feet, sub-divided into a central hall and several smaller chambers. Right round it the roof projects about 26 feet, forming a verandah, supported by columns. The roof is usually of corrugated iron covered with tiles, which are an excellent and cheap protection against heat. In a few of the huts corrugated iron has been used for the inside division walls, but the experiment has apparently not been very successful. All rooms have large bays, and the open space left between the two slopes of the roof ensures constant ventilation. Moreover, the climate makes it possible to keep all doors wide open. The 150 by 60 feet huts accommodate 43 men each. In the other quarters also the space is amply sufficient. The internees as a rule have a lot of baggage, and the piles of boxes, trunks and valises make many of the rooms seem crowded.

All inhabited quarters have the earth covered with a paving of squared stones. The only exceptions are two small rooms in a building formerly used as a store, in which the hard earth floor has not yet been replaced by one of stone. All walls are whitewashed. The buildings are excellently cared for, and spaced well apart. A number of fine trees afford shade here and there, while the recently made plantations and the many cultivated gardens near the huts show a wish to enliven the appearance of the camp. Some buildings were covered with climbing plants in full bloom.

Under the heading of furniture, the administration provides each internee with a bed, a table and a wooden arm chair. The interned are given all facilities for adding cupboards, shelves, easy chairs and anything else they may want, by ordering them from fellow countrymen in the camp who do joinery and upholstery.

The camp is lit by oil lamps at the cost of the administration. Inmates who wish to have additional lamps may obtain them by payment. "Lights Out" is at 10.30 p.m.

To complete this description of the housing accommodation we will add that the interned have full liberty to decorate their rooms with pictures, photographs, portraits of their sovereign and the German Generals, and with flags and patriotic emblems. . . .

The following is the official list of daily rations per man, for both interned people and the British troops on duty at the camp.

		INTERNED.		BRITISH TROOPS.	
Bread	...	453.6 gr.	(1 lb.)	453.6 gr.	(1 lb.)
Meat	...	340.2 „		453.6 „	(1 lb.)
Potatoes	...	226.8 „	(½ lb.)	340.2 „	
Vegetables	...	225.1 „		113.4 „	
New milk	...	113.4 „		——	
Tea	...	14.17 „		5.67 „	
Sugar	...	56.70 „		39.69 „	
Salt	...	14.17 „		——	
Pepper	...	.4 „		——	
Rice	...	56.70 „		——	
Butter	...	28.35 „		——	

For variety, 28.35 gr. of coffee are supplied instead of 14.17 gr. of tea, and 28.35 gr. of lentils in place of rice.

Most of the kitchens are staffed by 54 men, and are in separate buildings provided with all the necessary equipment. The head cook has had all openings in the kitchens covered with movable metal gauze to prevent contamination by flies, but often encounters the deliberate negligence of the internees, who will not recognise the importance to health of this precaution. Many of the kitchens have adjoining bakeries, which provide all kinds of cakes and dainties for payment. These bakeries are private ventures controlled by the administration with a strict eye to health. Work in the kitchens is performed by volunteers from among the interned, who are in this way enabled to earn good pay. Some of them are professional cooks. In each camp a committee elected by the prisoners themselves is given charge of the kitchens and of arranging bills of fare.

Rations are distributed at the following hours:—

8 a.m. *Breakfast.* Coffee or tea; rice; bread and butter.

12 noon. *Lunch.* Soup; meat; vegetables.

5 p.m. *Supper.* Soup; meat; vegetables.

We were present at the mid-day distribution and satisfied ourselves that the rations were ample and of good quality. Each man has his own spoon, fork, etc. Meat is provided every day. . . .

The pastrycooks in each section sell sweets and cakes. All other provisions can be bought at the section canteens, which are well stocked with all kinds of goods sold at prices fixed by the authorities and displayed on the premises. We were given a price-list of all articles sold. All the milk brought to camp comes from a Government depôt in the charge of the head doctor and controlled by the cantonment magistrate. It is of exactly the same quality as that provided to British troops and Europeans living in the neighbourhood. It is sterilised in the presence and under the direction of a skilled British overseer, and then placed in sealed vessels and delivered by a British employee to the head cook at each kitchen. This procedure prevents any possibility of it being contaminated or adulterated. . . .

Hygiene. An abundant supply of running water is delivered under pressure from a well 15½ miles from the camp. Every house is provided with taps. For safety's sake the water is boiled before being used, until a few months ago: now it is chlorinised and then dechlorinised chemically. The water is cold and non-laxative. The camp contains 130 douches, one for every ten prisoners. Washing water is discharged into a river some distance from the camp. Prisoners receive 3 lbs. of wood daily for heating water. . . .

Medical attendance. The camp medical service is under Lieut.-Col. Molesworth, who is assisted by two British captains and a doctor qualified to practise in India. Besides these, there are six British military doctors in the Ahmednagar cantonment who are called in to the prisoners if needed. Nineteen German orderlies are distributed among the three camp infirmaries and the hospital.

The camp contains three young German doctors who do nothing in the way of attending to their fellow-countrymen. We were astonished at this and questioned the doctors. We discovered that they demand the same freedom as is enjoyed by the British doctors, in return for their services. Since this request could not be granted, Lieut-Col. Molesworth dispensed with their services and forbade them to enter the hospital. . . .

The hospital is fitted up in accordance with modern requirements. Four wards are kept for the prisoners and a fifth will be equipped for the more comfortable accommodation of sick officers. The operating theatre contains the latest patterns of sterilising stoves and instruments. The analytical laboratory, used chiefly for examining the blood of malaria, the stools of dysenteric and the sputa of tuberculous patients, is equally well equipped. Dressings and medicines are imported from England and ordered from the central depôt at Bombay. Hospital patients have good beds with spring mattresses and mosquito curtains. Cases are classified according to complaint, and special orderlies and material are allotted to each category.

Death rate. The climate at Ahmednagar is one of the healthiest in India. The camp lies high. Coming from Bombay, the train passes through tunnels and over viaducts to reach the top of the Ghâts which command the western coast of India. We took particulars of the highest and lowest temperatures for the year 1916. . . .

In July, as the plague in its epidemic form had been identified in the town of Ahmednagar, the head doctor issued a notice, inviting all prisoners to be inoculated at the dispensary against this disease. No prisoner would be treated, so a circular was distributed giving details of the precautions to be taken against the bodies of dead rats. Soon afterwards the case of plague referred to above [in a passage not given here] occurred in Camp B. That camp was immediately cleared and its occupants were transferred for a fortnight to tents in Ahmednagar fort. As soon as the camp had been disinfected, the floors fired, the walls scraped and re-whitewashed, the furniture treated with cresol and all rat-holes stopped, the prisoners returned to their quarters.

Some meetings held to impress upon the prisoners the need of preventive inoculation resulted in 854 prisoners allowing themselves to be vaccinated; the rest refused. The epidemic plague was fortunately limited to a single case. . . .

Work. The prisoners at Ahmednagar are not forced by the authorities to do any work at all. All the men who follow an occupation do so of their own free will and receive payment. A kind of arrangement has been come to between the poor prisoners and their well-to-do comrades by which the latter give them work.

The camp authorities on their part take pains to afford craftsmen an opportunity of pursuing their trades by getting them orders from the people of the neighbourhood. Payment for orders executed is made through the camp accountant, who opens a special account for each workman and pays him the money in regulation instalments. We looked this register through and observed that quite respectable sums had been earned in this way by the prisoners. Among the craftsmen noted by us were garage mechanics, watchmakers, joiners, plumbers, frame-makers, tailors, a gunsmith, a piano-tuner, painters, photographers, etc. Every section has its hair-dressers.

Discipline. The relations between the commandant and officers and the prisoners seemed to be very good. Everything possible is done to lighten their captivity, either by giving them all the freedom compatible with the demands of discipline, or by avoiding anything that might cause offence. So far as the necessary obligations of a life in common permit, each prisoner occupies himself as he sees fit and to suit his own tastes. Some of the men devote themselves to gymnastics and sports; others cultivate a small garden; others, again, read, write or draw. Some spend their time in learning foreign languages. In Camp A there are skilled workmen who make all kinds of articles, some of them very artistic. Last year there was an exhibition of all these manufactures, most of which were purchased by the prisoners themselves. . . .

Disciplinary punishments. The disciplinary regulations are the same as those mentioned in connection with Sumerpur Camp, and, in fact, are identical in all Indian camps. The only modification in this case is to allow a prisoner punished by having his correspondence stopped, to inform his family of the fact, and of the duration of the punishment. The offences which have had to be punished are as follows: Drunkenness—formerly very common, but now reduced to one case a month on the average—quarrelling, talking with prisoners on parole, using invisible ink, theft, breaking into the canteen, etc. Most of the misdemeanours occur in Camp A, which contains many sailors and lower-class prisoners. . . .

Religious services. At Ahmednagar camp are several Benedictine monks who were missionaries in Northern India, as well as some Catholic priests and Protestant pastors. They hold services alternately in the premises of the Y. M. C. A.

Intellectual recreation. The prisoners have the use of a large building, which acts as theatre, two smaller theatre rooms, reading rooms with English papers, a well equipped English library, and a billiard room, which is open from 9 a.m. till 8.15 p.m. Singing and music is permitted. There are two orchestras, and many of the prisoners devote themselves to music.

There are many dogs in the camp.

All kinds of games are allowed. There are tennis and badminton courts. Card games, notably "bridge," are in great favour among the prisoners.

Letters and postcards. Prisoners may write four letters a month, two in German and two in English, on a single sheet of paper measuring four by seven inches. They must be in Roman characters. Any number of postcards may be sent, but, as the cards have very little printed matter on them, they are not very popular. There are no restrictions as to the number and length of postcards or of letters which the prisoners may receive. . . .

Until August, 1916, the British Government allowed the liquidators of German and Austrian businesses in India, in course of being wound up, to pay their employees and members 80-120 rupees a month. Since then this permission has been withdrawn, to the great annoyance of the persons interested, and as a result the number of people without means has increased rapidly. It is expected that it will be about 200 in March, and 300 later on . . .

In regard to the censoring of letters, which is done in the camp, we think that possibly some changes might advantageously be made. A single censor and two helpers cannot comfortably handle the correspondence of over 1,600 prisoners with despatch and all the care required. Up to a certain point we can sympathise with the strong complaints brought by the director of an important German bank against the way in which the censorship is conducted by a very young officer, who perhaps lacks the time and experience needed for a proper discrimination in dealing with correspondence. Some Germans who have been interned for nearly three years demand to be repatriated at once, or at least transferred to Dagshai, in the mountains north of Simla, whither the convalescent prisoners are sent in the hot season. Consul Ringger made a note of these demands, also of requests for permission being given to receive monthly sums from the liquidators of businesses in course of liquidation. The matter will be taken up with the Indian Government.

3. CAMP AT BELGAUM (BOMBAY PRESIDENCY)

Contained 214 interned civilians.

. . . *Situation.* This camp is a short distance from Belgaum town, which lies on the Southern Madras-Mahratta Railway, at an altitude of about 2,800 feet. The place is considerably colder than Ahmednagar, and is a sanatorium to which many people go for the hot season.

Belgaum is a civilian camp. The British call it the "family camp," as it is made up principally of households including children—until March, 1916, women and children only, about a hundred of whom were sent home, lived there. Later, permission was given to husbands interned in other camps to rejoin their wives at Belgaum.

The camp commandant is Colonel M. A. Halliard (on the retired list), assisted by Inspector Robinson, of the Police. The camp has been visited twice by the U.S. Consul at Calcutta.

The commandant seemed to us to treat his charges very kindly—one might say in a fatherly manner. The prisoners are not watched in any way: there are no sentries. The garrison consists of British soldiers. . . .

Housing. In the Alexandra section the prisoners occupy two large stone and brick buildings, standing on a plinth about 30 inches high. Round each building runs a verandah 11 feet wide supported on columns. A partition wall divides the building longitudinally, and the two parts are sub-divided into separate rooms by other internal walls. The verandah is also divided into sections by reed fences; so that each suite is a distinct unit made up of three, four or even five rooms, according to the number of its inmates. In front of the buildings runs a road 33 feet wide, on the further side of which are some small brick buildings which contain the kitchen and quarters for the native servants. Each suite has one or two of these buildings allotted to it; besides a bathroom. The larger families have two bathrooms. All living quarters are tiled, well ventilated and perfectly sanitary.

The authorities provide only indispensable furniture, such as beds, tables and chairs; but the internees have availed themselves largely of the permission to get for themselves whatever additional furniture they may desire. Each suite is tastefully and comfortably arranged, with pretty tables, chairs, carpets, pictures, bookcases and, in some cases, pianos. Green plants, flowers and small gardens add to the pleasantness of these quarters, which their occupants showed us with pride.

As far as accommodation is concerned, the folk interned at Belgaum may be said to fare as well as in a good hotel.

The Victoria section also is made up of perfectly healthy and comfortable buildings, erected on well shaded ground. The internees' messroom was recently given up to the British troops, so a new dining hall is being built for this part of the camp.

All these buildings had previously been used as billets for British officers and married soldiers. . . .

In the camp we partook of the lunch which is given to the interned, and found it ample in quantity, well cooked and of good quality. The interned may have as much as they like of any course. The refectory consists of three large rooms close to the camp office. Meals are nicely served, with a proper supply of table linen, silver, etc.

Quite a large number of families prefer not to take their meals at the mess. Some employ a native cook, who is paid by them and prepares meals to suit their tastes. In such cases the Government rations are augmented by provisions bought in the three camp stores, run by native shopkeepers. Other prisoners order their meals from the mess steward under an arrangement made with him. The extra cooks which this system requires are paid by the Government.

Children under three years of age receive 4 lbs. of milk daily: other children and adults the allowance fixed for all camps alike. An extra payment of 2 rupees monthly per head is made for meals served in quarters. . . .

Walks. The camp is unfenced and all the interned are free to take walks whenever and wherever they like; though, for reasons already given, the bazar and native quarter are out of bounds. Internees must be back in camp by 10 p.m. In the morning and evening there is a roll-call of men only. . . .

Disciplinary punishments. Since the camp was started (1 March, 1915) no penalties or punishments have had to be inflicted.

Correspondence. At the present time letters and postcards take about two months to reach Germany, and there are complaints of their often being lost *en route.* There is no restriction as to the number or length of the letters that may be sent or received. We saw some letters which ran into a dozen pages of close writing. Postcards with printed information are not used. On the average 30-40 letters and 12-15 postcards reach the camp weekly.

Money orders. Very few come from either Germany or Austria. . . .

Religion and recreation. Until 1 March, 1916, a Lutheran pastor interned at Ahmednagar used to come to Belgaum regularly to conduct services for the Protestants. He was then sent home with his wife, and since his departure the ladies of British origin married to Germans have attended the English church. The Lutherans have an American pastor who comes on Sundays to take services and often visits them during the week. The Catholics have a chapel in which a priest celebrates mass on Sundays and Fridays.

As the recreation hall in which the interned used to assemble has had to be given up to the garrison troops, a new one will be built, and a credit of 800 rupees has been voted for it. The prisoners hold concerts in their rooms. They have hired pianos and own some violins and other instruments. Good teachers have been secured for the children. There is a free English school and a German school charging fees. Tennis, badminton and cards are popular.

Relief. In December, 1916, the U. S. Consul at Calcutta sent 100 rupees, and in February, 1917, the Consul at Bombay 531 rupees, to be distributed among needy prisoners. Poor prisoners who apply to the commandant get a grant from the Indian Government of 30 rupees a month per head for adults and 15 rupees for children. In such cases no supplementary allowance for clothes is made. Clothing and footwear are the items of heaviest expense among the interned. About 20 families may be regarded as in poor circumstances.

4. CAMP AT BELLARY (BOMBAY PRESIDENCY)

Visited 12 March, 1917. Contained 137 Turkish prisoners of war.

. . . *Walks.* The Turkish officers in Bellary Camp, are free, as officers on parole, to take walks inside and outside the camp within a radius of 3 miles, between 6.45 and 11.0 a.m. and 4.0 and 7.0 p.m. As a sanitary precaution the bazar and native town are placed out of bounds. The roll is called in the morning and in the evening. Private soldiers may not go outside the camp except by special permission. . . .

Medical attendance. The sick at Bellary Camp are treated in the huge hospital which was built some years ago for British troops. This building is as remarkable for its fine architecture as for its splendid internal equipment. It is surrounded on all sides by wide verandahs, and has lofty, well-lit and roomy wards.

The head doctor is Major Shaw, I.M.S., who specialises in malarial complaints. He is assisted by a Turkish doctor, Capt. Faradj-Nareschah, of Bagdad; Capt. Gonsalvez, I.S.M.D., and an assistant surgeon, M. Subramanian. The Turkish doctor, who used to practise in Basra, speaks very well of his circumstances and treatment, which are better than those of native doctors with the same qualifications. Some native orderlies complete the sanitary staff.

A special ward is set apart for suspected cases, and an isolation ward—at present unoccupied—will deal with infectious diseases. There is a sufficiency of dressings, drugs and disinfectants. Any apparatus required can be got from Madras. . . .

Food. A contractor in the camp supplies meals to the officers, who have a choice of two scales. The first, costing 30 rupees a month, includes:

1. *Early breakfast:* Bread; butter; milk; tea.
2. *Breakfast:* A meat course; eggs; vegetables; bread.
3. *Supper:* A meat course; vegetables; mutton curry; a sweet course; bread.

The second, at 40 rupees a month, includes two more courses. Officers may also order extras. Some of them prefer to have their meals prepared from the rations by their orderlies. The messroom is very suitable for the purpose, and the table service leaves nothing to be desired.

Among drinks soda-water—whisky and soda—is most popular. By doctors' orders officers may buy three bottles of spirits—cognac, gin or whisky—per month. With this exception, sales of strong liquors are forbidden.

Canteen. The camp canteen is well stocked with foods and articles of all kinds. It is run by a private contractor, and a price list is exhibited. Any complaints about the canteen may be addressed direct to the commandant. . . .

The commandant and prisoners are on excellent terms. The latter informed us through two of their number speaking French and English respectively, that they were quite contented and had no complaints to make about their treatment. They hope that the commandant will continue to show them the same kindness, which is greatly appreciated.

Correspondence. Prisoners are allowed to write one letter per week in English and one in another language, length being unrestricted. Postcards with printed matter in Turkish are little used. Prisoners are entitled to receive an unlimited number of letters and postcards, but very few are delivered (70 in eighteen months). They all come from Sumerpur, the prisoners' old camp; none from Turkey. Most of the officers were captured in Mesopotamia, and seem deeply grieved at having had absolutely no news of their families, in some cases for two years. We advised them to send all their letters to the International Committee of the Red Cross, which will forward them to the Red Cross at Constantinople to be transmitted to their destinations. Postal communication with the Bagdad district is at present slow and difficult.

Money orders. The same reasons are no doubt responsible for the prisoners receiving no money from their families. The Red Cross has sent the following amounts to the prisoners at Bellary:—

4 March, 258.15 rupees; 7 and 9 March, 552.7 rupees.

Parcels. Only one parcel has been delivered since the camp was formed.

Religion and recreation. There are no priests among the prisoners, many of whom read the Koran and say their prayers. The commandant let them have some premises for their religious observances, but they preferred to use them as a café-restaurant.

Some of the educated officers read the English daily paper and three illustrated weeklies, which are sent to them. They will soon have an Egyptian newspaper, translated into Turkish. Some officers have asked that the Red Cross should send them a small collection of Turkish books. Music and singing are allowed. The favourite games are dominoes, chess and backgammon. The commandant put a football ground at the prisoners' disposal, but the game has not caught on.

5. DEPÔT CAMP AT CALCUTTA

Visited 28 March, 1917.

Prisoners sent to Burma by the British military authorities are taken by boat from Mesopotamia to Karachi, and thence by railway to Calcutta. As embarkation for Rangoon at Calcutta occasions some delay, a depôt camp has been formed there and prisoners spend one to four days at most in it.

This camp is in Fort William, the historic citadel of Calcutta, now used as a depôt for British troops. Large grass lawns, surrounded by fine trees, and forming three distinct sections, have been set apart for the prisoners in this huge enclosure. . . .

Medical attendance. Before prisoners embark at Karachi, they are closely inspected by the medical authorities. Any prisoners who show signs of illness or are obviously weak are detained there in hospital. Every boat transporting a batch of prisoners carries a doctor. Further, if the batch be a large one, a second doctor accompanies it to the place of internment. A medical inspection is held at the Calcutta depôt camp, and any sick cases are removed to the hospital for native troops.

6. CAMP AT KATAPAHAR (IN THE HILLS NEAR DARJEELING)

Visited 30 March, 1917. Contained 36 interned civilians.

Situation. The camp at Katapahar for interned civilians is near Darjeeling, in the Province of Bengal. The town of Darjeeling, situated on the lofty spurs of the Himalayas at an altitude of 8,000 feet in magnificent country, is the "hill station" of Bengal. The Governor and all his staff remove thither as soon as the hot weather renders residence in Calcutta too distressing. . . .

Housing. Katapahar station is on rocky ground with a step slope which ensures good drainage. The buildings are of square stone, carefully put together. Until lately they were used as barracks for officers and Hindoo troops. The roofs are of corrugated iron, and the walls are whitewashed inside. All rooms have wooden floors. Boarded verandahs are built out from most of the buildings. Windows are glazed and of sufficient size. A cemented gutter round each barrack drains away the rain-water.

The various buildings used for quarters are assigned according to the standing of interned families. Most of the bachelors have separate rooms, while some are put two or three in a larger room. Married people occupy two or three or even more rooms according to the number of their children.

Each suite includes a room with a fireplace and a bathroom. All quarters are kept clean and sanitary.

The occupants express complete satisfaction with their accommodation. . . .

Clothing. The authorities provide the prisoners with linen, footwear and winter and summer clothes. The clothing estimates for the whole year are got out in March, when clothes are examined and distributed. If necessary, internees may ask for extra clothes.

Relief. Most of the internees are sufficiently well off. The poor among them are allocated a fixed annual sum of £5. . . .

On returning to Calcutta we interviewed Mr. Edgley, Under-Secretary to the Bengal Government, and laid before him the points raised by the interned people at Katapahar. The requests related to:

1. Permission to buy spirits.
2. Permission to correspond in German with their families in Europe.
3. Extension of bounds for walks.
4. Reduction in the number of roll-calls (now three per day), and their abolition in the case of women and children.

All these concessions were granted us.

7. CAMP AT THAYETMYO (BURMA)

Visited 11-14 April, 1917. Contained 3,591 persons, nearly all of whom were Turkish prisoners of war.

. . . *Hygiene. Water supply.* The question of a good water supply has been most carefully studied. Colonel Fooks, I.M.S., head of the army medical service in Burma, told us at Maymyo that the Irrawaddy water, after settlement and purification with solution of chlorine, is quite fit to drink; but, although the whole native population uses the river water, the danger of contamination prevents it being used for camp purposes. Five wells are now being utilised. The water drawn from these at a depth of 26 to 33 feet, from a sandy stratum, is clear and cold. It has been analysed several times with very good results. The depth of water in the wells varies with the rainfall; it was 3 feet last year and 8 feet this year, in April. After the rainy season has set in the level rises about 20 feet and the wells meet the requirements amply. April and May are the low-supply season. Adjoining each well is a metal tank, quite enclosed, into which the water is delivered direct from the well by a rotary hand pump. cocks control the distribution.

The camp authorities recognised that the pumps now in use do not work very satisfactorily. Their mechanism is too delicate and, in the hands of the soldiers, often gets out of order, so that there is almost always a well under repair. Three large new tanks are now being made and will be kept full by pumps running all day long. Each holds 400 gallons (1,600 litres). In the future prisoners will not be allowed to fetch their water from the wells, as this caused crowding and disorder. The kitchens will be supplied by pipes straight from the tanks. Each hut has a tank holding 2 gallons (8 litres) per man housed. The kitchen tanks hold a gallon per head for preparing food. Every lavatory has four basins filled with water once or twice daily. Turkish prisoners did not complain of lack of water, but we think that the well-fitted shower-baths will be more used when there is a more abundant water supply. The effort made by the authórities to improve matters in this respect deserve the highest praise. There is a sufficient number of bathrooms and of laundries in which the prisoners wash their linen.

In the fort, which is occupied only by three sick cases and some attendants, water is drawn by hand from a well in buckets.

The two hospitals are provided with wheeled baths and fixed douches for the sick. The orderlies have their own special bathroom. . . .

In connection with sanitation we may refer to the question of poultry keeping, which is of some importance. Quite a large number of Turkish prisoners have taken up the rearing of fowls round their huts, and have made a good profit by selling the produce to the officers. The camp authorities have not discountenanced this minor industry, but, as the number of fowls increased too fast and disease broke out among the stock, poultry are now confined in a separate enclsure.

Exercise. The large area round the buildings of

the two camps gives room for all necessary exercise. A field 970 feet square is kept for games and gymnastics. Turkish soldiers seem to prefer sleeping to walking. They told us that the walks which they have to take in squads outside the camp are distasteful because their escort of native Reservists walk too fast.

Officers have free range within the camp, visit their club on the river bank, and can obtain permission to make excursions in the neighbourhood. For reasons of discipline and health, prisoners may not go to the town.

Clothing. Soldier prisoners receive free from the camp authorities:

1 fez; 2 white cotton shirts; 2 white suits; 1 pair of slippers; 2 pairs of socks; 2 pairs of drawers; 2 towels; 1 bathing wrap; 2 flannel jackets; 2 handkerchiefs.

At an inspection we found the prisoners' kits clean and well kept. We were told that at Thayetmyo, as in many of the other camps, kit is sold on the sly. Some representatives of the prisoners whom we questioned declared that the men were perfectly satisfied with their clothes. The shoes are good, though of various kinds, and wearers of Eastern slippers envy those of their fellows who have shoes. The soldiers carry in their pockets or under their shirts a small tin plate with a number in Turkish and European figures. . . .

Food. . . . Every morning the section sergeants and men on fatigue duty go to the hut where the rations are issued. The latter are in accordance with the usual scale and number of prisoners: and are handed to the food orderlies, who weigh them in the presence of the English sergeant in charge of supplies and take them to the kitchens. The beef which we saw was of excellent quality, and is supplied by a contractor who brings a certain number of cattle to camp daily. The beasts are not accepted for eating until they have been examined by the British overseer. As we received some complaints about the quality of the meat, the commandant gave orders that in future a Turkish doctor should be present every morning at the time of drawing rations and receive all complaints about the quality of meat and other provisions. Complaints are made on the spot by heads of sections, to obviate their being pút forward when it is too late to investigate them. The Turkish soldiers expressed a wish to be given mutton occasionally, and to have a larger choice of vegetables and a different diet during the Ramadan fast. The commandant promised us to do all he could to meet these requests. Mutton is seldom to be had in that district, and the British soldiers rarely get it.

The individual daily rations are as given on p. 19. Every prisoner receives 40 cigarettes and a box of matches weekly, and a pound of soap once a month. . . .

Medical attention. The camp medical service is under a head doctor, Captain J. M. Williamson, R.A.M.C., who is assisted by Lieut. Brookes and Surgeon Swolle. Seven Turkish doctors have practised in the camp since its formation, viz., Col. Bahidj Bey; Capt. Yosef; Capt. Mustapha; Capt. Mehemed Osman; Lieut. Suad, a dispenser; Lieut. Hamid Chakir, an oculist; and Lieut. Aghia, the assistant dispenser.

The Turkish doctors and Dr. Williamson accompanied us during our visits to the hospital and gave us much information. We were pleased to see that the Turkish doctors were on excellent terms with their English colleagues. The last were loud in their praises of the energy and devotion of the first, who get no pay beyond what they receive as officers. In return they enjoy a great deal of liberty and may go anywhere outside the camp. At the time of our visit two of them were on leave in Rangoon.

Death rate. During 1916 two officers died—Col. Subhi Bey from cerebral hæmorrhage, and the other from pulmonary consumption. There have been 76 deaths among the soldiers and civilians; which, distributed among an average total of 3,500 prisoners, are 2.17 per cent. Mr. Samuel G. Reat, the U. S. Consul at Rangoon, visited Thayetmyo on 26 March, 1916. His report gives an average death rate of 3.19 per cent., which he considers too high. Our opinion is that a considerable number of the deaths, which occurred during the two first months after arrival in camp, may perhaps be attributed to the exhausted state of prisoners from the front. The very carefully kept chart in our possession of the disease and death rates at Thayetmyo shows a decided increase after the arrival of each batch of prisoners. Deaths have been due to the following causes:

Typhus	1
Dysentery	9
Malaria	7
Pyrexia (origin unknown)	1
Pneumonia	3
Pulmonary consumption	12
Tuberculosis of various kinds	3

Exhaustion	4
Anæmia	8
Hemiphlegia	1
Heart trouble	4
Trombosis	1
Endocarditis	1
Bronchitis	2
Pleurisy	1
Nephritis	4
Enteritis	9
Piles	1
Hernia	1
Wounds	3

During the first three months of 1917 the number of deaths was 4, or a yearly death rate of 2.18 per cent. Deaths were due: to appendicitis, 1; aneurism of the heart, 1; enteritis, 1; sprue (choleraic?), 1.

The dead are buried with the rites of their religion in the presence of their comrades. The cemetery is well cared for. Officers' graves are apart from the rest.

Religion and recreation. At Thayetmyo camp the religious question has passed through several stages. At first the commandant proposed fitting up a building to be used as a mosque. The late Col. Subhi Bey, who had considerable influence over his fellow-countrymen, opposed the suggestion on the ground that the mosque would be abandoned after the war, and that this would be contrary to religious teaching. Later on, the Turkish prisoners asked to be allowed to attend services at the mosque in Thayetmyo town. But this request was not granted, as the higher authorities feared, not unreasonably, that in a country of numerous sects and violent religious hatreds, quarrels might be caused by religious ceremonial. We took the matter up both with the commandant and with a soldiers' committee called by us. The proposal to build them a place of worship in the camp was gratefully accepted, and the building is now in course of erection. An imam interned in the camp will be responsible for conducting religious services.

Intellectual recreations are thought little of by the Turkish prisoners; but card games, draughts and dominoes are very popular. An orchestra has been got together, and gymnastics and sports are much appreciated. On the day when we arrived we watched a gymkhana got up by the Turkish soldiers, in which jumping, running and wrestling events were keenly contested. We admired the strength and litheness of the athletes. Some money prizes were distributed amid the cheers of the onlookers.

Officers are allowed to arrange their own pastimes. They have a club in some pretty premises on the banks of the Irrawaddy, with billiard and refreshment rooms. They received us there with great cordiality. Some go in for painting, others for music. The lack of Turkish books is felt greatly, and we think that it would be a good thing were a committee in Turkey to make a point of sending out useful and interesting works. There is a fair number of books in French, English and German.

Correspondence. The prisoners despatch about 10,000 letters per month and receive from 2,000 to 3,000. Letters from Mesopotamia sometimes take four or five months on the way, while those from Constantinople come in five or six weeks. Prisoners may write two letters a week in any language except Hebrew. The War Office supplies regulation note-paper—a sheet measuring 6 by 10 inches, folded three times, the back being used only for the address.

Letters are at present censored in camp by a Mosul Syrian and two interpreters. Later on they will be censored at Bombay, to avoid loss of time. The censor, however, seldom has to delete passages in either outward or inward letters.

Money orders. The total value of postal orders received by the prisoners now amounts to about 1,200 rupees a month. A little time ago Turkish civilian employees who had not been paid up to date by their Government began to receive their salaries from Constantinople. Prisoners may receive in one sum any amount of money sent to them, excepting those whose conduct has been unsatisfactory. Anybody who wishes to leave all or part of a remittance on deposit is given a private bankbook in which credits and debits are entered. We were not able to establish how long it took money orders to reach the payee, as they show only the date of their arrival at Bombay. Some orders have had to be returned through being insufficiently or inaccurately addressed. To avoid this inconvenience, orders should bear the prisoner's number and the name and address of the sender.

Assisting prisoners. There is no committee at Thayetmyo to handle correspondence with relief societies. The following bodies have sent relief: the Red Cross at Constantinople, the Armenian, Jewish and Mahometan communities at Rangoon. The last has made some considerable contributions, chiefly among which are: 5,666 khaki shirts, 5,000 yards of material for clothes, 1,500 cigarettes, 99 boxes of soap, 480 aluminium cups, 1,200 rupees for soda water, 50 pairs of football boots, 6 footballs. In addition, 345 rupees have been sent for the school and sports; 1,000 rupees have been distributed among the civilians with the help of Col. Subhi Bey and 530 by Saifullah Bey. The Armenian community at Rangoon has contributed for the Armenian, Greek and Syrian prisoners 360 towels, 360 shirts, 492 handkerchiefs, 2 cases of soap, 32 boxes of cigarettes, 300 Bibles and 335 rupees.

The Jewish community sent cheese and other foodstuffs for the observance of the Jewish Passover.

The Mahometan community has offered to meet the needs of the poor, but up to date no calls have been made upon it.

Conclusions. The Thayetmyo prisoners generally look well and not at all depressed. They give a very good impression. We asked Saifullah Bey to arrange a meeting between us and representatives of the soldiers. It was held on 14 April, the only other person present being a Turkish officer who acted as interpreter. We noted, for forwarding to the British authorities, some criticisms and wishes which were laid before us. The men showed moderation and no ill-feeling. The authorities have met the men's wishes so far as is possible.

The camp commandant treats his prisoners with real kindness, doing everything to lighten their lot that his instructions permit. In this he is well backed up by his colleagues, who are on excellent terms with the Turkish officers. The last sent us certain demands which will be given serious consideration. Eight Turkish majors presented a separate petition, drawn up in violent language and making accusations which we knew to be inaccurate and misleading. We sent it back. On the other hand, we received a touching letter of thanks from the Turkish soldiers.

8. CAMP FOR CONVALESCENTS AT SHWEBO (BURMA)

Visited 18 April, 1917. Contained 90 persons, nearly all Turkish prisoners of war.

Situation. The camp is situated in Upper Burma, 125 miles N. of Mandalay and about 2 miles from the small town of Shwebo. It is a camp for convalescents. The climate, though hot, is dry and healthy, and one of the best in the country.

Prisoners who need a change of air are sent here from Thayetmyo for a month or two. The camp commandant is Lieut. H. Parry, who, single-handed, carries out most conscientiously the heavy work that falls on him. . . .

Exercise. From 7.0 a. m. to 6.30 p. m. officers may take walks without escort in the neighborhood of the camp anywhere inside an area 7½ miles in circumference. Private soldiers take exercise in the camp and twice a week go for walks under escort: though the walks are optional, and sometimes nobody falls in for them. Soldiers whom we questioned on the point allege that their shoes are not stout enough for the purpose.

Clothing. The regulations are the same as at Thayetmyo. The officers, who have to pay for their clothes, complain that the tailors' charges are too high. The only complaint made by the soldiers was that about lack of stoutness in their footwear. The military authorities, whom we approached on the matter, promised to look into it; but one must take into consideration the fact that for a year past footwear has been as difficult to obtain in India as elsewhere.

Medical attendance. The military hospital in the British cantonment at Shwebo is under Dr. W. N. Greer. One of its wards is reserved for Turkish prisoners; but contained no patients at the time of our visit. The hospital arrangements, the dispensary, materials for dressings and disinfection, and the sanitary service are in excellent order and leave nothing to wish for.

Sick soldiers attend sick parade at 7.30 a. m., officers at 5.0 p. m. As there is no interpreter in camp at present, Capt. Djavid Cherket always comes to parades. A wheeled ambulance is always available for carrying patients who cannot walk to hospital. Most of the Turkish officers are very emphatic about the improvement in their health due to the Shwebo climate.

9. NEW CAMP AT MEIKTILA (BURMA)

Meiktila was formerly the summer station of the British Government in Burma. The prisoners' camp was not yet in use when visited by the Commissioners.

10. QUARANTINE CAMP AT RANGOON (BURMA)

Visited 30 April, 1917.

On returning to Rangoon we were informed by General Young, commanding the Rangoon brigade, that a quarantine camp had just been opened for suspicious cases notified during the recent movement of Turkish prisoners. We considered it our duty to include this camp in our inspection, to inform ourselves about the measures taken by the authorities to prevent the spread of cholera. . . .

Water for drinking purposes is brought from Rangoon every morning in a tank boat. The pump on board is connected up by a rubber hose with the cast-iron piping which carries the water to the camp reservoir, whence it is distributed to all buildings. Contamination is impossible.

The patients number nineteen. Two are ill with cholera, and are housed in an isolated hut under the care of special orderlies. The kitchen and latrines of this hut are isolated also. Fifteen patients who showed symptoms of cholera are at present recovering and under observation. One patient is being treated for mumps, another for pneumonia. No deaths have occurred.

Transport. We were interested in getting some information as to the conditions under which Turkish prisoners are transported from Mesopotamia to Burma. We obtained it partly from the prisoners themselves, partly from the English doctors, and partly from the captain of the mail steamer Bangala, S.I.N.C., on which we left Rangoon, and which had brought in the last convoy.

There are two camps at Basra, an observation camp, and an isolation camp reserved for epidemic diseases. The prisoners stay in the first for from two to four weeks. Patients in the segregation camp remain there until they have recovered. When a convoy has been made up it is taken by steamer to Bombay or Karachi, and thence across India to Calcutta by railway. The men travel in carriages able to hold 60 persons. Biscuits, bread, cheese, fruit and tea are distributed twice daily during the journey. At Calcutta, the prisoners are either embarked at once or housed at Fort William (see p. 42) to await departure. Each convoy is accompanied by a doctor and the necessary staff. All boats used as transports are disinfected at the end of each voyage. The sea voyage from Calcutta to Rangoon takes three days, the normal time for mail steamers.

At Rangoon the prisoners are put aboard large flats—towed by steamers of the Irrawaddy Flotilla Co.—and taken straight to Thayetmyo. The journey to Meiktila is partly by rail. Officers travel first or second class according to rank. Special arrangements are made for kitchens, lavatories and closets on the steamers.

Each steamer is able to carry 2,400 persons, but the number of Turkish prisoners put aboard never exceeds 1,300.

II. CONCLUSIONS

(Translated without Abridgement)

Turkish prisoners. In the course of three months we visited all the camps for Turkish prisoners of war in Egypt, India and Burma. Nothing was kept from us. We had full liberty to inspect all premises, to examine registers, and to obtain all useful information. We were allowed to talk with the prisoners as much as we liked, either through an interpreter or directly in French, German, English or even Russian. After every inspection we interviewed representatives of the soldiers and of the officers. The camp authorities always made a point of not being present, so that the prisoners might have full liberty to lay their complaints before us. Prisoners were also permitted to send us letters and petitions.

We can therefore affirm that we know the exact position of Turkish prisoners interned in British camps. The premises occupied by the prisoners are either buildings normally used as barracks for British or native troops, or buildings erected for the purpose. In both cases the sanitation is excellent. The quarters and bedding are kept scrupulously clean; and special care has been taken over the fittings of the W. C.'s, lavatories and laundries, and the discharge of sewage and dirty water.

The feeding arrangements—of first importance to the prisoners—are liberal and practical. The rations are the same as, and in some ways larger than, those given to the British troops. The system of supplying the prisoners with the necessary materials and allowing them to prepare their food in their own way to suit their own tastes may be regarded as a perfect solution of the food problem in interned prisoners' camps. The complaints which we recorded related especially to lack of variety in the diet, a variety which can hardly be given when large quantities are in question and the local conditions are difficult. The camp authorities are very strict about the quality of the provisions supplied by native contractors. The Turkish prisoner is fed well.

He is also clothed well. Except for a few complaints about footwear, the Turks expressed themselves as satisfied with their kits. We think that the more or less compulsory carrying of a small identity disc is far preferable to bands, armlets, name tabs, etc., worn too visibly outside the clothes.

Bad treatment is unknown. Discipline is strict without being harsh, and the prisoners get on well with their guards. The penalties inflicted for infractions of discipline are reasonable, and are generally incurred by quarrels and petty theft, in a few cases by attempts to escape. There is no corporal punishment, and practically no compulsory work. Camp fatigues are light, being distributed among a large number of men. We know how difficult it is to organize workshops and yards, especially when one has to deal with men who know no trade and show little desire to work. The attempts made so far have been almost complete failures; but it will be worth while to keep the matter in view and try to establish employment, not for the sake of the return, but in the prisoners' interest.

The medical organization deserves nothing but unstinted praise. The excellent health of the Turkish prisoners is explained by the good condition of the hospitals, the abundance of surgical equipment and drugs, strict prophylactic measures, and the conscientious care taken by the doctors. Considering the exhaustion and weakness of the soldiers who come from the front and are in a state which renders them most susceptible to infection, it may be said that the disease and death rates among the normal camp population are as low as it is possible to keep them.

Difficulties in correspondence form the subject of many complaints. The delay of letters, parcels and money orders may be attributed to the serious difficulties on lines of communication. Postal relations with the East are affected especially, but this is not the fault of the British authorities.

The position of the Turkish officers certainly deserves our sympathy. In many cases they have no news of their families, they are without intellectual resources, and are divided among themselves by political differences; so they find it hard to resist the moral depression due to a prolonged captivity. Unhappily, they take little interest in the soldiers interned along with them. They should superintend the recreations and games of their men, and get up lectures, meetings and concerts, to which the British authorities offer no objection.

In all camps Turkish officers receive considerate and courteous treatment, and the British officers do all they can to keep on good terms with them. At Thayetmyo we dined at the commandant's table with Turkish officers, who were received as distinguished guests. Nothing pleased us more than this chivalrous behaviour toward unfortunate enemies.

We conclude this report with the expression of our belief that the Turkish prisoners, on returning to their country, will testify that England has treated them with all the humanity they could wish for.

2. *Interned German and Austrian civilians.* Complaints—not to call them demands—were most numerous in civilian camps. It is easy to understand that people who have lived many years in India, occupying independent and in many cases distinguished positions, and are accustomed to good living, find it very hard to be dragged away from their business and reduced to a confined and monotonous life. Their connections are broken, their interests suffer, and in many cases future prospects are more or less prejudiced. Most complaints related to affairs and not to the climate, to which everybody is accustomed already. The British authorities do all they can to make things better by treating the prisoners with the greatest possible consideration. Witness the fact that all the requests which we laid before the Indian Government to assist the interned were promptly granted.

Many of the interned took an unprejudiced view of the situation and assured us that in the circumstances they had nothing but praise for the consideration shown them by the authorities.

The Delegates of the International Committee of the Red Cross:

(Signed) DR. F. BLANCHOD.
F. THORMEYER.
EMMANUEL SCHOCH.

Made in United States
Troutdale, OR
11/03/2026

56844683R00040